CW00815721

BEYOND THE
IMAGINATION
A COLLECTION OF POETRY

YoungWriters

EDITED BY CLAIRE TUPHOLME

First published in Great Britain in 2010 by:

 Young**Writers**

Remus House
Coltsfoot Drive
Peterborough
PE2 9JX
Telephone: 01733 890066
Website: www.youngwriters.co.uk

FOREWORD

Here at Young Writers our defining aim is to promote the joys of reading and writing to children and young adults and we are committed to nurturing the creative talents of the next generation. By allowing them to see their own work in print we believe their confidence and love of creative writing will grow.

We are proud to present our latest collection of poems that we are sure will amuse and inspire. Given the high number of poems we received, the selection process was a very difficult task yet the energy and enthusiasm put into all of the entries ensured that we enjoyed reading each and every one. An absorbing insight into the imagination of the young, we hope you will agree that this fantastic anthology is one to delight the whole family again and again.

CONTENTS

Bowlish Infant School, Shepton Mallet

Coit Friends Club, Sheffield

Corona Secondary School, Nigeria

International School of Geneva, Switzerland

Lindley Junior School, Huddersfield

Weelsby Primary School, Grimsby

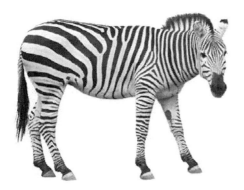

THE POEMS

My Mum

M y mum is good
Y ou do nice things

M ake me nice dinners
U sually you play games
M y mum is the best.

Alec Brown (8)

I Want To Be A Queen

I aspire to be a queen of accuracy, agility and adroit to attain accolade.
I believe in becoming a queen of benevolence, benign and bonafide to beget bliss.

I crave to be a queen of calibre, cachet and capability to collect credit.
I desire to be a queen of decency, decorum and dexterity to derive Dame.

I'll enjoy becoming a queen of ebullience, ecstasy and exuberance to exude eminence.
I foresee becoming a queen of fidelity, flair and flamboyance to fetch fame.

I'll be glad to be a queen of gallantry, glamour and grace to gain glory.
I hanker to be a queen of holiness, honesty and humility to have honour.

I intend to be a queen of integrity, incorruptibility and invincibility to inspire inspiration.
I'll joyously be a queen of justice, je ne sais quoi and joviality to jot joie de vivre.

I'm keen to be a queen of kismet, kindness and kahuna to kolekt kudos.
I long to be a queen of legality, largesse and luminescence to last-ditch la dolce vita.

I mull to be a queen of majesty, magnanimity and munificence to muster magnificence.
I need to be a queen of novelty, niceness and ne plus ultra to nest up nobility.

I'm obsessed in becoming a queen of omniscience, oomph and openness to obtain Oscars.
I'll be proud to become a queen of panache, probity, and prominence to pick up paean and prestige.

I quest for the quiddity of a queen: A 'Queen of Queens', a queen of quintessence and a queen of quickness to quantum leap in quality.
I'll relish becoming a queen of rectitude, resonance and righteousness to receive renowned reputation.

I seek to be a queen of sagacity, sapience and selfishness to secure success.

I tend to be a queen of tenacity, talent and trustworthiness to take trophies.
I want to be queen of ubiquity, urbanity and uniqueness to uphold universal unity.
I vow to be a queen of vision, virtue and veracity to harvest victory.
I want to be a queen of wonders, worthiness and wisdom to wrought wondrous works.

2

I yearn to be a queen of yardstick and youthfulness to end up a Young Turk.
I want to be a queen of zeal, zest and zeal-ot-ry like Queen Elizabeth II of
England.

Triona Uwem

The Change Of Changes

The sun popped up from his bed of clouds
and shone, to brighten up the morning.

The moon looked down in disgrace to find people
spying on him with a telescope.

A star launched itself towards Alaska
granting wishes along the way.

The sky kept the clouds as slaves
his evil plan to flood the world!

The sea became angry
and charged towards the land

A stone skimmed gracefully along the water,
until he crashed and drowned.

At 12 o'clock the night was completely gone,
but came back at 8 for its revenge.

The mountain couldn't afford a hat
so its summit always got cold.

The dawn had to get up early
to awaken the rooster.

The morning was so tired it didn't wake up
and the man was late for work.

The evening couldn't wake up, but he wouldn't want
to spoil the lovely summer's day.

Daniel Grummitt (11)

Darkness - A Silent Scream

Feeding my grief with their pain
The harrowing wind and rain
Consuming the light from my soul
The darkness from the black hole

The poison spreads throughout
backstabbing, an unheard shout
The eerie light the moon doth deliver
Makes you quiver, your spine doth shiver

Consumed in a cloud of rage
Your body doth grow old with age
The words, the cackles of the demons resound
By cords of antipathy you are bound

Trapped in the middle
The resounding riddle
The hurricane of emotion
You're trapped at the eye

Don't think about shouting
Escape you are doubting
Here nothing is heard
Not even your cry.

Pippa Barrett (15)

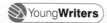
 YoungWriters

The Painting On The Wall

Upon an iron nail
In the gallery hall
Hangs proudly with a second view
The Painting on the Wall
For that is what it's called
It was painted without title.
The Painting on the Wall we call it.
It has no specific meaning,
No secret message or hidden item.
Its meaning is nothing yet something.

The fine brush of paint,
The clashing colours that shouldn't make sense but do
Mixed, overlapped, melting into each other,
Reaching out to the onlookers,
Pulling them into confusion
It was painted without title.
The Painting on the Wall we call it.
It has no specific meaning,
No secret message or hidden item.
Its meaning is nothing yet something.

It could be waves of passion,
A maze of life
Choosing the right paths
Meeting dead ends
Coming to decisions
Then finding the way
Out of pain, struggle and fear
There is only one way in and only one way out.
People walk right past it,
Not giving it a second glance
They say it's a phoney
A painting of nothing,
They don't give it a chance.
They don't see its uniqueness,
They don't look beyond the paint
They don't see what I see
I see a picture painted with passion and feeling.
Love, pain, strife and loneliness,

No one sees what I see.
It is like life.
We are only human and so we judge a person by their looks,
We assume a man is dangerous by the hunch on his back.
We steer clear away because of the look in his eye and his crooked teeth trying to smile but results in a sneer.
We do not see what he feels inside,
We judge that because of his outward appearance, he's imperfect.
But on the inside he has meaning, passion, hopes and dreams that want to be free.
He's just like you on the inside, but it is hidden by what we see on the outside. We fear him because he is different, because he is not perfect to our standards.
But who are we to judge?

The painting is different from the rest,
Although it may not be the best;
It has meaning and reflects our lives,
Of how the average being strives;
And though I see an abstract masterpiece
Hanging proudly in the gallery hall,
I can't make everyone see what I do.
Everyone walks past it,
They just see a Painting on the Wall.

Hadassah Miriam Shah (12)

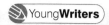

The Sunlight Of Easter

I looked outside my window
and remembered straight away
it's Easter time, let's enjoy the day!
Now the time for games and fun around
as flowers bloom,
no more snow,
the sun is shining,
we search for Easter eggs
and enjoy them with a feast!
Make hot chocolate that's fun!

Isabella Molinaro (9)

Scarlet Rose, My Baby Sister

The night she came I will always remember
The snow lay deep on that cold December
From the day she came home I have never felt alone
The shadow that is my baby sister

She smiles, she laughs, she giggles at me
And usually she eats all of my tea!

Some mornings she wakes me with a slap on the cheek
And then she wants me to play hide-and-seek
But she never realises that I always peep when we play hide-and-seek
Oh, I'm glad I have my little baby sister.

Louis Parr (10)

My Cousin, Scarlett

My cousin Scarlett is as sweet as can be
She may be a pain but I know she loves me
My cousin Scarlett she loves to eat
She may not be able to speak
But she loves to giggle at me.

Megan Conder (10)

So Can You

My favourite person is Metin Akpinar
He is an actor, my favourite actor
I have been watching him on TV since I was 6
He's great at teaching lessons if you need one, he sure can do
He is like a factor, he loves helping others and he helps all of us
He may be Turkish, but he is human like us
So don't worry, he won't eat us
He is like a shining star
But he is not like any other star
He's brightly coloured and he is overflowing with colour
Metin Akpinar is his name, you might not know him
But that's his name
I look up to him, so can you
He may be old but he's wiser than you!

Ilayda Tuncel (11)

YoungWriters

My Moma

My moma is so lovely
She gives me lots of money
Which I spend on sweets for my tummy
Yummy, yummy, yummy.

I'm like a queen when she's around
She is like a Ferrari racing through town
She puts on anti-wrinkle cream to make her look young
And one of her dogs has a problem with his lung.

She goes to church to praise the Lord
I bet if I went I would get bored
Her hair is like the sunshine shining so bright
She doesn't need to turn the light on in the night.

She lives in a cottage next to the road
When she goes shopping she brings a big load
Black is her favourite colour, I don't know why
When she puts it on she looks like a spy.

She has lots of tea sets which she puts on display
She only gets them out when I come to stay
She has lots of mobile phones, which she gives to me
She is like a charity shop, but I get things for free.

Alannah Ball-Wood (9)

My Fab Dad

My favourite person is my dad
He shares all my problems when I'm sad
For many reasons, my dad is the best
Better than all the rest!

I can't go to sleep without a sweet dish
Even though sometimes I forget to feed my fish
At night when I feel myself fright
My dad always appears straight away, in my sight.

My dad taught me how to ride a bike
Me and my dad like to go on very big hikes
Me and my dad like to play football and basketball
Although sometimes I get clumsy and I fall.

He is my inspiration
Takes away all my tensions
He is my role model, I envy him very much
He is the best in the world
Best in the universe
The best that ever existed before my dad
. . . Just like my mum!

Talvin Singh Rana (10)

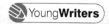

The Pet Shop

Come to the pet shop, what can I see?
I see a puppy dog looking at me.
Hello little puppy dog, what can you say?
Woof, woof, woof, all of the day.

Come to the pet shop, what can I see?
I see a kitty cat looking at me
Hello little kitty cat, what can you say?
Meow, meow, meow, all of the day.

Come to the pet shop, what can I see?
I see a parrot looking at me
Hello little parrot, what can you say,
Pretty polly, pretty polly, all of the day.

Come to the pet shop, what can I see?
I can see you and you can see me.

Lia Harding (7)

Yes, You Dog!

Yes, you dog!
Who jumps on the sofa
And tears it to bits when I'm out.

Yes, you dog!
Who jumps on me
When I return and makes bruises all over my body.

Yes, you dog!
Who gobbles your food
And splatters it everywhere.

Yes, you dog!
Who makes my daughter scream
Because you chewed the ear off her teddy.

Yes, you dog!
Who jumps on my feet at night
And feels like an elephant lying there for 3 hours. (No sleep.)

Yes, you dog!
Who howls at five in the morning
Keeping me awake for two hours.

Yes, you dog!
Who first thing in the morning
Pounces on my slippers.

Yes, you dog!
Who brings in a dead bird each morning.
Yet at all of this, how come I love you?

Phoebe Haywood (8)

Dreamland

Complete and utter chaos
No one moving
Everyone is still - yet the world feels full of anarchy
All you can hear is crying
In Dreamland.

Everyone is smiling
Dizzy with excitement
No reason for it except
It is summer and all is well
In Dreamland.

Bees talk
Pigs fly and most of all - don't forget
To lock up all your books
Or they'll fly away
In Dreamland.

Some people say they've been to Dreamland
Others deny its existence
One thing they all agree on is that
People think of great things
In Dreamland.

I must say goodbye - I am tired and ready for a visit
To Dreamland.

Emma Yeo (14)

What I Think Of Your Touch

When I think of you
My heart skips a beat or two
Yet every time it happens
All I can do is think of your touch
The way your warm hands touch my skin
Then when you pull away, my skin tingles still
It's as if your soul reaches into me
And dances with my own
Yet all you really did
Was touch me for a brief second
That I will remember
And cherish forever.

Charlie Shute (15)

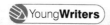
A Noisy Fear

On noisy nights
On noisy days
I make a wish and think of you
A noisy dog
Which is my noisy fear
And a silent wish that you were here!

Nazhm Tanveer (10)

Angels

Angels are made out of light
They are so beautiful and they are so bright

Although we didn't see them
Hold on tight

They move as fast as lightning
Sometimes they are so brightening

You will see them by your grave
But don't be scared, be brave.

Samia Ahmed (9)

Days Like This

I stare at the computer
Nearly done
I sign my name in a flamboyant flourish
And push myself away from the computer
After throwing myself on the nearest item of furniture
I sink into the warm, soft covers of my bed
Staring into the lampshade, dreamily
I dance on the carpet
'I'm free, free!'

How beautiful the world is on days like this
The wind, nothing but a whisper, among the trees
Laughing at their secret joke
Teasing me
Telling me I can't play
But I don't mind.

How beautiful the world is on days like this
When the sun welcomes you
Into its sunny embrace
Petting you
Telling you, 'Not to worry.'
But to watch how brightly it can shine
It shows off a bit
But I don't mind.

How beautiful the world is on days like this
The snow gently, calmly floating down
As gracefully as the angels who sent them
They threaten to fall on you
And make you shiver
Suddenly they swerve
What little, cheeky, innocent-looking tricksters they are
But I don't mind.

How beautiful the world is on days like this
The rain dripping
Creating a soothing lullaby
As you fall gently into a deep sleep
It comforts you like a mother's voice
Cleanses your mind of all negative
Or impure thoughts that might hurt you
Sometimes it gets too loud
But I don't mind.

How beautiful the world is on days like this
The leaves have fallen
Creating a carpet for only me
They crunch as my boots, step carefully on them
I like the sound it makes
They remind me of a new clean break
Soon to come
The caramel-coloured leaves
Sometimes
Mask something not-so-nice underneath
But I don't mind.

Come to think of it
The world is beautiful, no matter what type of day it is
It is just hard to see that through the struggles and problems
Through everyday life
But as a wise man once told me
'We should be grateful we have problems,
it shows us we are alive,'
So, oh Lord, I am grateful I am alive. Are you?

Francesca Amara Lewis (12)

School

I love school, oh yes I do
Going to school is a must too
I like going to school, how about you?
They say geography is now good for you.

School is there
School is a cheer
As you can see
School is a wonderful place to be.

School, school, school
School dinners how can I explain?
The custard is lumpy
The gravy is sloppy
School, school, school
I feel sick, get me a bucket quick
Oh, too late, I've been sick!

Hannah Mendes (10)

Untitled

Is there a reason why I'm still breathing
When this Earth I'm slowly leaving?
They say when you're born you're slowly dying
Is that why when you come out you're crying?
Life is a ride with joy and sadness
Sometimes you end up running round in madness
Life starts small with a glimmer of hope
But a few years down the line your parents can't cope
But one thing you should never forget
Is to never ever regret.

Temiladeoluwa Olugbenga (13)

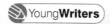

Bullying

Bullying, bullying, it's a horrible thing
The bullies think they'll always win
But they won't because we are here
We need to stop bullying every year.

Cyber, physical, verbal are types
But that will stop because we all have rights
Here is a story of what bullying is like
Such a story can happen most nights.

'Stop, stop, you're hurting my leg,'
Said 11-year-old girl, Susie-Meg.
'Why, why are you bullying me?
Where are my glasses? I can't see.'

'Susie, Susie, where are you?
I'm taking you to buy some new shoes.'
Said Susie's mum who didn't know
About the bullies at school, Sam and Joe.

'OK, Mum, I'll be there in a second,'
But Susie was looking for her lost specs
When Susie came back wearing her new shoes
She went to show her best friend Lou.

They went off to play in the park
But after a while it was getting dark
Susie lived one way and Lou the other,
'Come on, come on,' shouted Lou's mother.

So Lou went off skipping along
Singing to herself a happy song
Then there were footsteps, all of a sudden
Of scary people, running and running.

Running towards Susie faster and faster
Susie knew this would end in disaster,
'Come on, Susie, it's time to come in.'
'OK, Mum, I'll be there in a min.'

'Susie, you are just a four-eyed freak
And you are a weak little geek.'
'Stop it, stop it, I've had enough
You are just bullies because you are rough!

I'm ringing Childline to help me out
You'd better run otherwise you'll get a clout.'
And so the bullies ran away
They were so ashamed, I'm glad to say.

Susie realised what to do
When they come back she'll scare them through
That brings us to her end of the story
So when you need help ring Childline, make the bullies sorry!

Sofi Sheppard (12)

Raindrops

A waterfall of screaming tears
From the almighty clouds above
Falling from the heavens is a frightening job
Pitters on the rooftops and patters on the ground forming streams
Lakes and rivers all around
The starlight opens and shines on me
And shows thy beauty that lies within me.

Ian Ryan (11)

Sam's Poem

Long, long ago when the Earth was blank
No one ate and no one drank
Until one day 'Osa' in the sky
Said to himself, 'An idea have I,
I'll make an Earth where my sons will live
And to each other a gift I'll give.'
Some chose magic, some chose tools
Some chose lightning . . . but they were fools!
When everyone had chosen a gift, there was just
The youngest who heard a swift
It was a bird next to his ear who said to him
With a grateful cheer, 'Get a shell.'
So he got a shell and tipped it around,
Sand poured out without a sound
Until one of the sons said, 'Look at that.'
Everyone looked and started to chat,
'That is marvellous, that is good.'
Everything looks how it should
And finally when the sand had stopped
Everyone stood looking shocked,
'Please give us land, please give us land,'
So he gave them some of his beautiful sand
So he gave them seeds to plant some trees
He also gave them a few IDs
Everyone was happy and they all sang
That was how the world began!

Sam Murray (9)

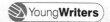

God's Power

The winter is approaching
There's a hard bite to the air
The autumn leaves are dulling
And the wind blows through my hair.

I look up to the moody skies
Of swirling windy greys
A swooshing, moving world of cloud
Obscures the bright sun's rays.

The cloud, it seems an angry force
Of raw and emotional power
An ancient nature's force at work
Of thunder, lightning, shower.

Electricity bolts through the sky
A thunderclap is heard
I gaze up to the sky and sigh
It's a very magical world.

For I cannot impress upon you
The power I sense and feel
When I see such emotion in nature,
I tell you: God is real.

Jordan Holmes (16)

A Single Touch

One single touch
And they know
How their life must go.

One single breath
And they see
How they can be free.

One single kiss
And they forget
About reality.

Two separate hearts
But they mustn't be apart.

For they may be different
But one similarity
They shall be together
For all eternity.

Charlotte Lauren Higgins

Summer

Summer, summer's nearly here
Watch the cold disappear
Let the sun shine on me
As it glistens on the sea.

Summer, summer's nearly here
Everyone's best time of year
Lick an ice cream all day long
Or even sing a joyful song.

Summer, summer's nearly here
Everyone's down by the pier
At the beach or on a boat
You don't even need a coat.

Summer, summer's nearly here
There's no need for a tear
Be happy, dance so joyfully
Invite all your friends round for tea.

Summer, summer's nearly here
Everyone begins to cheer
People bathing in the sun
All the children having fun.

Olivia Bromage (8)

My Night Alone!

I'm all alone and it's cold outside
I sit in the shadows trying to hide
The street lamps dim then suddenly light
This all looks strange at the dead of night!
I hear the rustle of fallen leaves
And then the stir of the outside trees
The moon tries to shine brightly up high
While the fog is determined to cover the sky!
I hide under my duvet, my heart beating, beating fast
I must make the most of tonight for it might be my last
But the clock is ticking, it's one now, I'm scared
Look out of the window again, I haven't quite dared!
So I turn on the TV and try to smile
It's impossible so my mum's number I dial
There's a message there waiting, waiting for me
It was sent at twelve especially for me
It said, frightened, scared, fearful do not be
The message my mum sent for me
She said she'd return before the sky turned black
But you see the thing is my mum never came back!

Holly Miller (11)

Special Easter

Where did innocence go?
When did the confusing turmoil begin?
Why did He have to go to His teacher, God?
I say sadly it's not His fault.
From my eyes came salty tears
I couldn't stop calling His precious name
Watching at a distance, no more tears to cry
Royalty reduced to a bow
Why did He have to die?
Where did love disappear to?
When will it return again?
Look at what He strolled
Through to make me live again
Where are You now my precious Hero?
Are you still there in my heart?
I want You to be in my loving heart
You taught us to follow in His precious way
He showed me the way, the truth and light
But not to fight.
I love Him and I will follow in His way
Easter is not all about cute bunnies and stuff
But to be funny
Easter also expresses everything I can be
But following upon His name
It puts the people who don't believe
In Him to shame.

Albin Arulgnanaratnam (9)

The Polar Bear Alone

Is that a polar bear standing alone out there?
Is that a polar bear soon to be so rare?

What used to be ice caps
Where he could fish, play and romp
Are shrinking to icicles clinging like bats.
Once he was regal and so full of pomp
He used to be happy. Frolicking and fishing
His home is now smaller, soon to be no more.
He stands upright, proud and keeps wishing and wishing
No family, no friends, he is frightened to the core.

Is that a polar bear standing alone out there?
Is that a polar bear, does nobody care?

Joshua Ball (10)

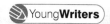

Groovy Gran

Here she comes
There she goes
Don't even think that my gran strikes a pose.

What're you doing?
Where did you go?
Going on an errand, that's what I know.

Caravans here
Pontins there
Ripping her hair out for us everywhere.

She is the best
You would agree
I would kneel down on my knee
Just to say, 'I love you so.'

Chloe Lianne Croxon (11)

Under The Sea

I put on my aqua-lung and plunged
And dived into the sea
Down, down, down, I went
To see the beautiful seaweed.

A mermaid like a silver ghost
A starfish shining bright
I thought my eyes were going mad
But they were really right.

As I kept on swimming
I saw some wonderful things
A shark, a dolphin, all those things
But something caught my sight.

I thought to myself, what could it be?
So I went over to see
Oh my gosh, it shone so bright
It was round, just like the moon.

When I was done under the sea
I went back to my home
And showed my family
The massive golden coin.

Mairead Aitken (9)

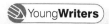

The Cheetah

The cheetah was sleeping under a tree
To keep in the shade from the scorching heat
A zebra quietly walked straight past
But the cheetah heard and woke up fast.
She zoomed across the scorching sand
Gracefully skimming across the land.

Soon it was the end of the day
But the cheetah had not caught her prey
A great big eagle hovered in the sky
And the cheetah watched him so beautifully fly.

The eagle landed on the ground
The cheetah heard the delicate sound
She quietly sneaked to where the eagle stood
And suddenly pounced like a cheetah would.

If you long to know what happened next
It really is such a dread
The cheetah did not eat the bird
The bird ate her instead!

Lucy Melrose (8)

My Animal Poem

We are trapped in a cage with nowhere to hide
All the animals come to me and confide
All of us are feeling the same
Each one of us are feeling the pain.

One day I was in Africa hunting, wild and free
Now everyone is staring at me
I am trapped in a giant goldfish bowl
Everyone is looking at me, it's taking its toll.

Now every day feels the same
I don't like this boring game
I was once the king of the jungle
But now I've taken a very big tumble.

But there are perks of living in a zoo
And that the keeper picks up my poo
I see children smiling, having fun
I wish I could do that, it's all right for some.

Rhiann Gay (12)

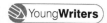

School Behind Doors

I don't like school at all
The gym really pongs
The teachers scream every time
When you're doing nothing wrong.

The finger pointed at you
When you're not the chatterbox
While everyone's outside, I'm inside
Detention is the worst.

Mum and Dad don't understand
What I'm trying to say
Before that they blow a gasket
Will someone listen to me today?

I really hope and wish
There is someone today
That understands how I feel
And lightens up my day.

My biggest issue is
I get bullied at school
The bully is plain mean
And his gang are just cruel.

I don't have the courage
To stand up for myself
I hope I can overcome my fear
And make someone proud.

Now all I need is someone
And a shoulder to cry on
It's really hard to find one
At the moment I have none.

Behind the doors of school
There is so much going on
Can happiness enter my life
Or will I stay undone?

Thasin Choudhury (12)

Host

It's time to say your prayers; it's time to say goodnight
It's time to shut your eyes and hope I don't visit tonight.

Why do you quiver with terror as I hover above your bed?
Why do you scream when I whisper, 'Next time I see you, you'll be dead'?

Do you expect to escape certain death because you run?
Do you assume that I can't get to you if you hide in the midday sun?

If you think begging will help you are deadly mistaken
If you think people can hear you, there's no one for you to awaken.

There is no longer time to explain
There is nothing left to do apart from inflict pain.

Now I'm human again, my new life I must not waste
Now I'm leaving the scene with great haste.

Next time my human form withers away
Next time my flesh begins to decay.

I'll move on and boast
I'll move on but never die as I use you as my host!

Eileen Hagon (14)

The Way Of Joy

Joy is like a bubble
Carrying you high above the clouds
Consuming your very being
Giving you a smile
It makes you be able to laugh
And sometimes shed a tear
Until someone or something bursts your bubble
And you come crashing through the air
And crash on the cold hard ground
With no one to pick up the pieces and convert you
The joy is left to bleed from your broken heart
But then someone or something refills and heals
Your once empty and broken heart
And time repeats itself again and again.

Niamh Darling (14)

Winter

Winter is cold, winter is freezing, winter is all around
Winter has snow, winter has Christmas
Even though
Winter has stars in the sky . . . they are so bright!

I put on my coat, gloves and hat
And I wonder . . .
Do I look funny in all that?

I walk in the snow: *crunch, crunch, crunch*, I turn
Back to see my footprints following me.

Playing in the snow with a hop, skip and run
Although it's freezing, having so much fun!

Hip hip hooray, it's never the same
Winter is here again.

Georgina Walsh (6)

Sleep!

Pirates sleep in the night
So there'll be no fight
But in the day they like to play
Under the shade of the sun's rays
For days and days.

On the ship they have a foal
It has made a great big hole
It's not a horse of course!

George Howells-Watt (9)

Animals

Monkeys and panda bears
Shooting them makes me scared
Frogs and kangaroos
I hate them being killed, don't you?
Zebras and vampire bats
Cheetahs and big cats
Grey wolves and crocodiles
All types of reptiles
Without them, our world is plain
Killing them is no fun game.

Aoife O'Toole (12)

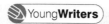

Kellogs The Corn Snake

Kellogs the corn snake, there is none finer
Than my hodgepodge patchwork corn Carolina
With scales so supreme and a checkerboard belly
When he smells his prey he quivers like jelly
Oh, when his forked tongue flicks for a second so short
To when he is so discreet, when he cannot be caught
Kellogs the corn snake, there truly is none finer
Than my hodgepodge patchwork corn Carolina.

Ella-Rose Gover (10)

The Inevitable Orphan

Two bears were locked in battle,
Fighting for the last bit of meat,
Their claws scratching; cutting with every swipe.
Suddenly the mother bear fell to the ground
Panting, breathing, as if every breath would be her last.
Then it struck the cub, if her mother died
Would she survive?

Eloise Hepburn (11)

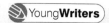

Costa Del Sol

The warm sunny breeze on my face
Entertainment like never before
The sea lush and cool as I dive in
The hotel room luxury and paradise
As we leave we say hi to everyone we see.

Michael Sutcliffe

Our Special Earth

Our Earth is very special
As special as can be
Though it isn't the closest planet to the sun
That's . . . Mercury.

It's not the hottest planet
That's Venus . . . The Evening Star
It's not the biggest planet
That has to be . . . Jupiter by far.

It's not the smallest planet
That's . . . Pluto, cold as ice
It's not famous for its reddish tint
That's Mars to be precise.

But Earth's alive with animals
With flowers, grass and trees
And best of all our special Earth
Is home to you and me!

Devika Tandon (10)

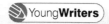

Atlantis

The lost city of Atlantis sank beneath the waves like a stone
And it was located in the Atlantic
Hence the name Atlantic Ocean.

Its walls were made of precious metal
With architecture so advanced that some say it was not managed
Today people say it was full of treasure.

Atlantis took up a whole island
It sank below the sea due to volcanic activity.

Some say it didn't exist
While some say it did exist and
Want to find the lost city of Atlantis.

Tim Myton (12)

Aberystwyth

I had a dream about Aber
the sea deep and blue
the sand soft and gold
I wasn't allowed in the rock pool
so I did as I was told.

Deep blue waves splashing up me
onto my sparkly pink bikini
I dried off straight away
then walked down to the bay.

I bought some ice cream
and found some crabs
Mum and Dad said, 'Well done,
go get the tea and kebabs.'
And then the magical world of . . .
Aberystwyth ended.

Elizabeth Dobson (13)

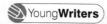

Unspoken Words

I sit alone
I dream alone
waking to see the same thing
the same four walls

My hands clutching my head
staring at both doors, both handles
listening to hear nothing
watching to see nothing but doors with their handles

My walls are sweating
the heat is rising
the walls are ready to burst
I need to be free

The doors are shaking
I lie awake ready to break free
I press my finger softly against a brick and feel it trembling
that's when I knew my walls were ready

They finally burst
cement, brick, everything flying everywhere
air getting to my lungs, I cry in happiness
I'm free at last, nothing can stop me now

I am free.

Katie Jane Jones (15)

A Tale Of Two Roads

We look forward
As the next generation
We strive to understand
Where the world is turning to
Where we are being led
By our past, the generation before us
A future with no religion as a border
One where all is equal
A future where peace prevails
One where it is the only way
I am not sure, for now
Where this road will take us
But it seems a much longer way
To the place of peace than the road
We chose not to take
The road of harmony with nature
The road of acceptance
A road where the news we watch
Is only filtered by the screen on each TV
Our future is in our hands now
Time is running out
And it's not too late to change lanes.

Haimanot Haile (17)

Naughty But Nice

Sweet, creamy, strawberry, sticky
Cheesy, crumbly, crunchy, licky

Tasty, delicious and yummy
A big slice of cheesecake for my tummy

After tea my tummy rumbles
For some cheesecake my tummy grumbles

Adding cream as cold as ice
Isn't it naughty? But it is nice!

Chloe Jobling (11)

She Dances In The Wind

She dances in the wind
Not a single sound
Delicately she lifts her feet
Into thin air
She sways here to there
Mesmerising everyone
A twirl here and a kick there
As she freestyles her way
Nothing more beautiful I have seen
Even as she floats in the atmosphere
Tired, the wind calms down
And everything comes to a halt
But as the wind blows gently
She moves more gracefully
She moves with the wind
With her soul she dances
Slowly and quietly it builds up
Then the wind is rushing
She dances
She moves
Rhythmically to the beat of the wind
The wind is taking her away
There she goes
But she will dance
As she dances only in the wind.

Shivani Sharma (13)

The Boy In The L

As the air fills with children's screams and laughter
Coloured eggs fall all around
One little boy stands out from the rest
With a big L on his chest
A little basket by his side filled with foil to catch your eye
Blue, red, green and pink, every colour that you think
Eggs are here and eggs are there, foiled eggs everywhere
Easter shouts and Easter screams are never quite what they seem
Chocolate mess and chocolate fuss, every adult shouting, 'Hush!'
At the end of the day when every child's too tired from play
It's nice to sit and lay, in the nice, hot, beating sun
Knowing the children have had their fun.

Toni Ashley Casteel (15)

Open The Door

I see a blank page
Appearing on the page
When my hand goes over it
Is a new world that can be
Whatever I aspire it to be
Open the door
To my imagination
The gateway into my mind
Lose myself in my thoughts
Make my dreams
My own world
Open the door
I see a wonderland
Of my own thoughts and dreams
An ever-changing world
Of my own creation
Of my own mind.

Chloe Forrester (12)

Spineless Love

Heartbreak is like a warning of sin
It's a cost that found a way to bring
Payment, of hurt to be happy like mankind
My heart has fear . . . life's cruel to be kind

Bleeding for a while
Spine like love . . .
(Spineless love)
Bleeding for a while
Under or above
(Get me over your love)
Bleeding for a while
Nothing but a thorn
For tame or for wild?
For I'm still torn.

A heartache is like a thorn lost within
It's lost but found its place under my skin
Lonely, but happy to hurt me while I'm high
We started here, but we can only end with goodbye
(We end with a tear)

Bleeding for a while
Spine like love . . .
(Spineless love)
Bleeding for a while
Under or above
(I'm over your love)
Bleeding for a while
Nothing but a thorn
For tame or for wild?
For I'm still torn.

My heart isn't worth breaking . . . anymore
Once, twice, three times . . . or maybe even four
One start with never an ending . . . but now it's law
Once, twice, three times . . . or maybe even four.

A heartbeat is like a number we can't control
It stops if there's nothing to make it a whole
But look, my heartbeat has no math, my break is no price
Why do we pay through hurt or aches, not only once or twice?

Bleeding for a while
Spine like love
(Spineless love)
Bleeding for a while
Under or above
(I'm over your love)
Bleeding for a while
Nothing but a thorn
For tame or for wild?
For I'm still torn.

Victoria Hanks (18)

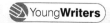

Freaky Ghost

F airly see them
R eally freaky and spooky
E erie things happen but nobody knows what
A round and around you look to check there's no ghosts
K nocks and bangs scare your mind
Y ells and screams freak you out

G hosts make you really scared
H ands are covered in bright red blood
O n your mind you have scared thoughts
S print and run, lots of ghosts are chasing you . . .
T ime is night-time so ghosts are everywhere!

Ellie Green (9)

The Power

Power striking
Again and again
Rising
Showing holes in the defences and
Closing up before you had a chance to weaken it.
It would fall back repeatedly
And miss every feeble punch they threw at it
It was strong

Even in its vast size it was ten times quicker than them
Those weak defenceless humans.

Caroline Macro (11)

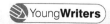

Dyslexia

Being in a dreamy world
Is an escape from words echoing in my ears
Jumping and twirling
Words sometimes falling into a dark black hole.
Letters and numbers, scramble and jumble
Across the page.
Must train them to stay still
Black print and bright colours on white paper
Hurt my tired eyes.
Concentration, confusion,
Headache
Voices become faster
Questions run into each other
Blurring
- Cannot look and listen at the same time
Overload, too much, switch off, daydream
. . . Escape into an imaginative world . . .

Mark McKenzie (10)

Charlee

My brother, well what can I say?
He does everything his own way
Wii, Xbox and PS2
He will always beat you
Blond hair, blue eyes and chicken legs
'Mummy please,' he always begs
1, 2, 3, 4 and 5
All these years he's been alive
Not very tall and not very fat
I think he is a little brat
Wears his glasses all day long
Always wants to sing a song
Always reads a book at night
I say, 'Mind the bugs don't bite!'
Charlee JJ is his name
Annoying me is his game.

Sam Cowan

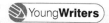

Happy Birthday

Great tidings to you my friend
May you prosper in all you do
May the Almighty grant you long life and prosperity
The doom shall never befall you

Great men, great things
They just do not achieve this in a day
But through diligence
Of course not.

The heights by great men reached and kept were not attained by sudden flight
But they, while their companions slept, were toiling upwards in the night
Great things start from minute deeds
May you and we all achieve this.

Abdul Fattah Fatoki (12)

The Sun Shines On Me

I wish the sun shines on me
and everything is good forever.
Look at everything around you
Everything beautiful
Look around and see.

It is a brand new day today
everything will be okay.
It is a good time and so
will be tomorrow I pray.

David Raeper (7)

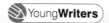

Faeries And Piskies

In a magical place not far away
The woodland faeries came out to play
But as they prepared for their summer sleep
The swamp piskies stopped counting sheep
They heard the screeching, frivolous noise
Of the faerie girls and faerie boys
They woke up and were red with rage
And planned to lock the faerie queen in a cage.
'That'll teach them,' the piskies said
As they smirked and crawled out of bed.
So in the dead of the midsummer night
The piskies laughed and gloated in spite
As they bound and gagged the queen
And sneaked out the palace, quiet and unseen.
In the morning the faeries were in a temper
As they heard the piskies snicker and whisper.
The faeries stormed from their faerie palace
And glared at the piskies with loathing malice.
The faeries and piskies stood on the grassy green
And in the middle sat the caged queen.
They fought all night and all day
And soon realised it was not war, but play
The piskies released the queen with smiles
And sat and laughed and talked awhile
But soon summer ended and winter reigned
So they waited for summer to do it all again.

Monika Ryll (16)

Winter

Winter's here, it's come at last
Christmas comes with a great big blast
Snow comes down with a blanket, soft breeze
Animals hibernate like birds and bees.

Trees in houses, decorations too
On a cold winter's night a warm sheet will do
Curling up by the fire in the dawn
Making a dream of Christmas morn.

Santa on the roof in his sleigh
Bringing you presents for Christmas Day
Listening for bells as they go to bed
Toddlers dream about Christmas in their sweet little heads.

Bethany Leanne Parker (10)

Powerful Ghost

He will haunt you,
He will eat you,
He might just pretend to greet you.

He's as big as a giant,
He's as strong as a tree,
He's as scary as something
That could kill you and me.

He will get you at night
He will get you at evening,
He will get you anytime
You dare to believe in!

Amy Stainton (7)

Daring And Dreaming

I dare to dream,
Of a world of pure peace,
Where terrorism, suffering and violence will cease.

I dare to dream,
Of becoming a star,
Having a mansion, a butler, a car.

I dare to dream,
To roast a sausage on the sun,
To find a huge diamond which weighs a ton.

I dare to dream,
Of a time I'll never fear,
When spiders and monsters are far from near.

I dare to dream,
That one day I will,
Look back on my life from Heaven's window sill.

I will see effort, happiness, love,
Also pain, hardship, no sign of the dove,
Whatever I see I know I'll be proud,
So long as I have dared to dream.

Bryana Aimble-Lina (13)

Friendship

I will always be beside you
until the very end
wiping all your tears away
being your best friend
I will smile when you smile
and feel the pain when you do
and if you cry a single tear
I promise I will cry too.

Fateha Begum (13)

Ladybug

Beautiful ladybug
You fly in the sun
Red and spotted
You look like a fairy in flight
As spotted as a leopard
You make me feel like a giant
As big as a bus
Beautiful ladybug
You make me think of a little red berry.

Amielia Frances Adlington (10)

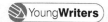

If I Could Be A Captain . . .

If I could be a captain
I'd sail the seven seas
I'd never do a spot of work
I'd eat the finest cheese!

If I could be a captain
My ship would be bright pink
Jewels and pearls would adorn the walls
And my ship would never sink!

If I could be a captain
I would rob people as I go
I would be extremely rich
But foes, I'd have, I know!

If I could be a captain
My sailors would do as I please
I wouldn't have to pay them much
And they'd never be as rich as me!

If I could be a captain
No one, to me, would say, 'No!'
For I would be a famous captain
And my name would be Jacqueline Sparrow!

Ellice Marie Hetherington (11)

A Friend

A friend is someone you can trust
A friend is someone by your side when it's hard
A friend is someone you can sometimes disagree with but still be friends
A friend is there till the end
A friend is your friend forever.

There is nothing more powerful than friendship and love
You don't have to worry, your friend is there always
A friend can make you happy
A friend can give you joy
You have all got a friend.

Declan Whatmough (10)

Guardian

G uaranteed to be with me forever
U seful and helping me whenever I need them
A nd protecting me from every little hurt, to
R emind me that the world is a good place
D eath feels harmless because
 I know they're there watching over us all
A nd guiding me in difficult times, and they
N ever let me down.

For my two guardian angels
And the rest of my family
With love, from Shona.

Shona Jain (13)

The Shipwreck

Deep in the depths of an undersea realm
Fish swim close to the rotting helm
Enough hideous beauty to overwhelm
Is found upon the shipwreck.

It lies against a background of teal
Accepting the harsh truth to be real
A hundred tons of wood and steel
Are found upon the shipwreck.

It fell from grace and left the sea
The magnificent vessel that left the sea
Now lies amongst its own debris
The once proud shipwreck.

Callum Morgan (13)

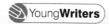

Paradise Lost

The waves roar
The tide crashes
The thunder booms
And lightning flashes
Down beneath the treacherous storm
A ship lies sunk
Bodies lay all around the mossy
Green vessel
Children and adults, memories and lives
Gone in the bounce of the tide
Families broken
Families devastated
Memories lost
Hauntingly still
The ship stays entombed
Like the humans all around it
Resting at the bottom of the sea
No Heaven, nor Hell
In paradise lost
Cocooned
In their underwater kingdom.

Katie Donoghue (11)

The Success Of World War I

Passing afar the dreadful odour of death,
Unable to hear my own heart beat,
Contemplation of memories, satisfied my breath,
By no means, have I yet been closer to defeat.
The explosion of bombs and shadows of planes beyond me,
Alas, not a soul so far has announced the decree.
I was fighting for my country's honour and liberty,
But now, my closest friends left have numbered to only three,
And when my country declared the war was complete,
Some soldiers remained still at war till he died
But I was the lucky one, who was given a treat
To go back home, content and full of pride
For the allies had won the war with great dignity
With the help of Russia, Serbia and France
Winning a big chunk of prosperity
All was worthwhile, as everyone was given a chance!

Mahbuba Begum (14)

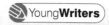

The Ride

Round and round I go
It goes incredibly fast
Zipping and zapping, rivers flow
There I go with a blast.

Being thrown from side to side
My mother's face is green
Now we go with a glide
To a place never seen.

Now I have to shout,
'Jo's wet his pants again!'
Hold onto your belt
We've gone insane.

Here it comes to an end
Because we're going west
Now we have crossed the bend
That was the best!

Katrina Reynolds

My Best Friend

He is as cute as a puppy
He is as fast as a leopard
He has big brown eyes like chocolate buttons
He is my best friend
He is Adam.

Brooke Leyla Williamson (7)

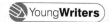

My Favourite Person

He is so sweet like a fresh strawberry
He is cute and cuddly like a kitten
He is like a best friend to me
We do everything together
We always make each other laugh
He has only been in my life for one year
I couldn't imagine life without him
My favourite person is my little brother, Kian.

Chloe Bateman (6)

Daddy

Daddy is the best writer ever
Daddy is kinder than ever
Daddy is beautiful
Daddy is loving and he loves me so much.

Ryoni-Natalya Markham (7)

My Favourite Person

My favourite person is Dad
He never makes me sad
A father who is funny
Is as sweet as honey.

At the moment I got my first bike
Dad is who I like
We always have so much fun
He is my number one.

Everyone is equal
In his words and mine
The world will never be fine
I wish Dad was nine.

We live in the same house
We're both louder than a mouse
The neighbours get very cross
That me and Dad are their boss.

Oh, how I love my dad
He never is bad
When he is happy
I am glad.

So let me wave my flag!

Hafiza Maria (9)

Untitled

She is as funny as a chimpanzee
She is as beautiful as a butterfly
She is as nice as a princess
She is my mum.

Connor Clarke (7)

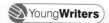

My Favourite Person

She is as wonderful as a child
She is as beautiful as a sun rising
She is as kind as an adult
She is as fantastic as a good reader
She is my sister, Niama.

Nawal Hersi (7)

My Favourite Person

My favourite person is my brother, Jaye,
I like him because we play.
We play in the garden.
When he burps he always says pardon.
He plays animals with me a lot
The best bit is when I get shot.
I come back to life because I have magic powers
Then we would walk back to the town
With lots of houses and giant towers.
We have lots of fun.
Then we pretend to go to the seaside
And then we are done.
I love my brother, Jaye
And he loves me right back.

Rhianna Spence (7)

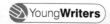

Ashlea Bates

I have a very special friend
I have known her all my life
We always have fun together
We are best friends forever
Ashlea is her name
We do everything the same
We always have great fun
Playing out in the sun!

Amy Green (7)

All About My Sister

Me and my sister are very special
Because we are twins
We dance, we go to Brownies
And swimming together
My sister does her best in everything she does
Because she has bad legs
I help her very much
Especially when she falls over
She is a star
She is fantastic
She is the best.

Amy Jones (7)

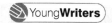

Madison

M y little sister is annoying as a blister
A nd she is the best sister in the world
D ancing is what she loves
I love being her big bruv
S illy games we love to play
O n a lovely summer's day
N ow she copies what I say.

Zachariah Shea Duffy (7)

My Favourite Person

He is very funny
He is like a clown
He can sing like a parrot
He can dance like a dog
He can shout like Dad
He can swim like a fish
He has got no hair
He shows his underwear
Comic book boy.

Oliver Scarth (7)

Steven Gerrard

S uper striker
T remendous attacker
E xcellent sports
V icious long shots
E ager emotions
N ever gives up

G reat teamwork
E xtra good free kicks
R iveting headers
R unning for goal
A wesome captain
R ushing down the left wing
D ribbling skills, superb.

Sam Hopkin (9)

Amazing Aunty Karen

A mazing Aunty Karen
U nderstands me
N ew Zealand is her home
T ogether we have fun
Y ippee, she has come to stay

K nows how to make me happy
A nd is beautiful
R eally nice
E xcellent at everything
N ever forget her visits.

Daisy Harvey (7)

David Villa

D eadly in strike
A stonishing long shots
V icious in attack
I maginative passes
D efenders' nightmares

V ery intelligent player
I ndestructible strength
L ethal left foot
L eft foot long shots
A nd only one.

Nikos Tokos (9)

My Cat, Salem

She's got greeny-yellow eyes
She has got black fur
She has a silver collar
And I like to hear her purr
Salem makes me smile
When I play with her
She is my best friend.

Emily Kara Oldfield-Cherry (6)

I Love Him

He's as nice as my mum
He cares for me
He is there for me
And he's my dad!

Megan Carter (8)

My Special Sister

She's the only one I've got
She loves me an awful lot
She aims to please
But can be a tease
She's cute as a bunny
And sometimes she's funny
Who do you think she is?
I'd love to kiss her
'Cause she is my big sister.

Alexandra Trill (6)

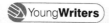

My Mum

My favourite person is my mum
She's very cool and lots of fun
She keeps my house nice and neat
And makes me yummy things to eat
She makes me happy when I'm sad
And tells me off when I am bad
She buys me gifts like toys and sweets
She plays games with me and gives me treats
She isn't great at playing football
But Mum is my favourite person of all.

Emily Given (10)

My Dad, Best Mate

My dad is fab, I've got to say
Makes me smile every day
Football, Lego, we play it all
He gives me a kiss if I have a fall
We both like fishing
We've been on a boat
He's the best dad in the world
I give him my vote
He works very hard
And I love him so much
Needs to shave a bit more
'Cause it hurts when I touch!
He protects me from all the things that I hate
My dad is fab, he is my best mate.

Charlie Peter Wain (6)

My Brother

My brother is my favourite
He is really funny
I always make him laugh
By tickling his tummy.

My brother is my favourite
I will like him for evermore
Oh, the adventures we get up to
They are never poor!

My brother is my favourite
He is really cute
He listens intently
As I play the flute.

My brother is my favourite
He is my only one
I'll always be his best friend
Until my life is done.

Sarah Megan Goswell (9)

My Favourite Person

My favourite person is Chelsi
She is very funny
She has a big tummy
But she is still very funny
She has a nice mummy
She is also so funny
And when she makes me laugh
It tickles my tummy
I like Chelsi
And her mummy
Because they are just so funny.

Elise Heydon (7)

My Sister

As stormy as thunder
As laughing as a clown
As crying as rain
It is my sister, Shreya.

Nisha Patel (6)

All About Katherine

She's as kind as a fairy
She's as pretty as a flower
She's as friendly as a dolphin
She's as playful as a kitten
She's as helpful as a teacher
She's my best friend, Katherine.

Isabel White (6)

Grandad

G randad is a lovely man
R uns me in the car whenever I want
A nd when I need him he is there
N ever ever lets me down
D evoted he is to me
A lways lends me a helping hand
D ivine and special in every way

That's my grandad to me.

Adam Evans (9)

My Great Dad

My favourite person is my dad
And his smile makes me very glad
He used to sneak biscuits up to us in bed
And he helped us grow sunflowers by our garden shed
He's the clever one in our home
But it hurts my hair when he brushes it with a comb
He's very funny and makes good jokes
And sometimes with the garden hose us he soaks
When we're on holiday the rules are different, he declares
Which means we all get to eat ice cream and chocolate eclairs
He sometimes teases me and hangs my teddies from the ceiling fan
And he once threatened to put one in a frying pan
He sometimes tickles us until we almost cry
And he'd hold us up in the air and we'd pretend we could fly
That's why he's my most favourite person ever
And whatever happens we'll always be together.

Olivia Railton (10)

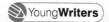

My Favourite Person

My favourite person is nice, clever,
Caring, loveable and the beauty is on her
She's the best ever since I was two
Right to the point I was first on the loo
Even when I had a spot
(I was so glad it wasn't a wart).
But sometimes she embarrasses me
Just like yours will do to you
But you just can't get cross with her of course
(Even if you have to cope)
Because you love her and you know she loves you
So now try and guess who it might be
I'll count to three and I will tell you
1, 2, 3 . . .
It's my cute mum.

Magenta Rose Kitson-Perfitt (9)

My Floppy

My Floppy is white
I hold him tight
We snuggle up together every night
I love him and he loves me
Because he's a part of my family
My Floppy
My bunny
My teddy
My friend.

Gracie Tina Clarke (6)

Mum

Mum you are a star so bright
You lighten up my days
Though words are not enough to show
How much I want to praise.

Mum you are a blessed gift
Given to me from above
You are the one I would die for
You are the one I love.

Mum you are my guardian angel
The one who's taught me right from wrong
You are the one who makes Heaven on Earth
You are the one I look upon.

Mum you are so patient and strong
You stay firm on your feet
Still you are so gentle and caring
You make my life complete.

Mum you are the words in my song
The melody I cannot forget
You are the one who understands my feelings
Who I tell secrets to and don't regret.

Mum you are the one who comforts me
You are the tree I lean upon
You are the one who makes it OK
You are the shoulder I can cry and rely on.

Mum you are the greatest thing in my life
You are my night and day
You are the one who I really care for
Even this poem is not enough to say.

You are my friend, my heart, my soul
You are the bestest friend I know
Though you might not be much for some
You are my love, my life, my mum.

Alisha Megan Sehdev (11)

My Little Sister, Libby

We play tea parties together
Dolly here, teddy there
We do anything together
Whatever the weather
And we both have long hair.

We're only two years apart
Her best colour is green
And we both love art
She is the best sister you have ever seen.

Her favourite meal is all the roasts
And sometimes we pretend we are hosts
And Libby likes playing on the slide
And we love to seek-and-hide.

Katie Chennells (8)

My Dog, Beau

Beau is very fluffy
He thinks food is very lovely
He loves the fridge
And he loves to go walkies over the bridge
But he doesn't like getting wet
He is my best pet.

Libby Chennells (6)

My Nephew

His name is Samuel
And he's 14 months old
He's a fun-loving boy
Who always brightens my day.

He's sweet and kind
I'm glad he's mine
My nephew
Forever and ever.

He loves bathtime
It's so much fun
Splashing and splashing water
On everyone.

He gives everyone their own little nickname
Which we all enjoy
I have just one last thing to say
Proud I am to be an aunt to a great nephew.

Precious Olagunju (10)

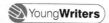

My Brother

Fast as lightning, dumb as a troll
My elder brother acts like a 5-year-old
And he is always cruel.

Years of torture and treacherous work
Watching over me like an evil hawk.

Names of cruelty, transforming into violence
Unlocking the doors into my gauge
Trying to find my flames of rage.

Although he's bad, we had good times
Laughing, making jokes, having fun . . .

Time passes, incidents happen
Like the one when I fell from 6 feet high
He came rushing, not even changing
Making sure I was all right.

Crunchy, crispy, bitter outside
But inside soft, sweet . . .
Looking out for me, bringing me joy
He is there for me, always there
He is for me, the one and only

He is my favourite person . . .
My dearest brother, Arnob.

Granthick Barua (10)

My Favourite Person Riddle

My mummy
I am
Fun
Happy
Nice
Kind
And
Pretty, who am I?

My daddy
I am
Silly
Funny
Bonkers
And crazy, who am I?

My sister
I am
Nice
Kind
Good
Funny
And
A Brownie, who am I?
Who are all these people?
They are all my favourites.

Jemima Crossey (5)

My Nan

I love my nanny
She is no ordinary granny
Frances is her name
Loving is her game.

She hugs me when I'm blue
Her heart so pure and true
Tells stories before bed
I love her as I've said.

This poem is to remind you
Of special things in life
She is a nan, mother and wife
I love you forever, Nan
As you can probably tell.

Abbie Murphy (14)

My Dad

My dad is the best
He always helps me with a hard test
Who works hard to earn money
My dad, he is as sweet as honey
My dad is very kind
He has such a brilliant mind
My dad works hard day and night
I always see him in my sight
It is a mystery
When it comes to history
He is always there to help me
My dad is the best . . .

Ishraq Choudhury Tasnim (10)

My Special Person

He's coming
Any moment now
I feel his presence in this place
He only comes at Christmas
I'll have you know
But he's my special person, so off you go
He's fun and bubbly, big and cuddly
Clever and kind
But anyway, he's my special person, so off you go
He also brings me presents
Anything I like
When I was eight he brought me a guitar
But don't you go thinking he'll do the same for you
Remember, he's my special person, so off you go
He is really famous, everyone knows his name
But I knew him first, and he likes me more
So go on, off you go, he's my special person
(He told me so).

Natasha Muzembe (13)

My Great Gran

Who is my favourite person?
My great gran, that's who.

I hope she's still here when she's 102
All her family love her lots
She is the best great gran I have got.

When I go, I'm never in the way
She waters her flowers every day
She drinks lots of tea and is nearly 93
I love my great grandma
She really is a star.

Thomas Morgan (6)

YoungWriters

Crazy Daddy

Daddy is sometimes funny, he tickles my tummy on the way to school
He went to 'Help The Heroes', I think he is really cool
Sometimes he is very, very, very, very, very crazy, that's boys
He likes eating barbecues and sometimes plays with my toys
I sometimes drive him mad by pointing out his hairy mole
We like to play football and we fight about who goes in goal
But he always picks me up from Brownies and holds my hand around town
He is the best daddy you could have ever, ever found.

Annabella Crossey (7)

Pixie

Pixie Lott laugh
Pixie Lott fun
Pixie Lott has loads of fun
Singing, chatting, running around
Dancing, prancing all about
Your smile is bright
And your songs are fun
That is why
You're my number one.

Amelia Moira Mosby (8)

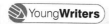

Someone Special!

Dancing along the riverside
In the sunset orange glow
But was it meant to be
Why did he go?
Where did he go?
It was all so big to me
Something we had was special
The feeling will never fade
It's more of a memory now
I know he's always out there
Just a message away
Now he's gone, but the feeling has not
So I know it will all be OK.

Bethan Knapper (14)

I Love The Countryside

I love the clean, fresh air
I love the way the dew lingers on the top of a leaf
I love the way the woodcutter lumbers his way though the woodland
With a tarnished, silver wheelbarrow and thick black boots
I love the tranquillity, peace and quiet
I love the way the stream just meanders through the village
I love the way the rusty tractor's engine sounds, as it goes through the fields
I love the way the wind circles around me
As I chase the cocker spaniel around the garden
I love the way the thick ivy spreads around the pebbled wall
I love the way the church bell sounds in the distant hills
I love the birds chirping faintly in the woodlands
I love the ripples my feet make as the fish underneath massage my feet
I love the way my wellingtons squelch as I trudge though the mud
I love the docile look the cows give me as I pass the opposite field
I love the narrow pathways that the thick overhanging brambles overlook
I love the countryside.

Nicole Lawrence (15)

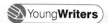

Jess, My Best Friend

Me and her we're joined at the hip
I feel like I've won the lucky dip
To have Jess, my best friend
Who never drives me round the bend.

Football is 'our' favourite thing
Jess, my friend, plays right wing
We both got picked, for county trials
My friend, Jess, she can run for miles.

Her and me, we're into the latest
Music from our favourites
On my birthday, she took me to JLS
My friend, Jess, she is the best!

Ashleigh Hollick (11)

Jacob

He is funny
He has googly eyes
He is a friend of mine
He has a thin head
And that is why
He is my best friend.

André de Bere (7)

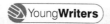
YoungWriters

Grandpa

When I was angry or upset, he would cheer me up
My lovely grandpa would buy anything for me
I remember giving him a big hug
I am upset that he is gone . . .
Who will make me happy now?
I remember . . .
My grandpa's sweet smile
I loved to see it all the time.
I remember his sweet voice
I remember
Him showing me how much he loved me
He loved me more than anything on Earth
I remember . . .
When he would ring up and say, 'Goodnight Nav,'
In his lovely sweet voice
I loved it when he gave me a kiss
He loved it when I gave him one too
Every night, I can easily picture his gorgeous image
When I am in bed, I think and dream about him
All the time . . .
I miss you Grandpa
I miss you!

Navjeet Singh Bhogal (11)

Grandpa

I remember . . .
When he used to pull my ears
Whatever I wanted, he would give it to me
Especially sweets
He would tell me jokes and make me laugh
Thank you Grandpa!

He was . . .
Good to spend time with
Excellent Grandpa to make me laugh
Always got me what I wanted
Never hurt me, even when I did something wrong
(Or very, very, very bad, he was always with me)
Always made me laugh
When he told me jokes, I got the giggles!

Arjun Singh Bhogal (9)

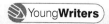

My Childminder

Debbie Duck likes cooking and makes lovely cakes
Her home is like a farm, full of friendly, funky animals
Jadie-Boy, the cat, is ginger and stripy
Evie, the dog, is white with brown spots
Dotty, the duck, is simply white all over
There is also a horse by the name of Ocean
And when Debbie goes riding she becomes a 'Duck on the Ocean'
All of Debbie's children chatter like chipmunks
They love Debbie dearly because she is so much fun.

Eleanor Hill (7)

My Favourite Person

Eric is little, Eric is chubby
He sleeps quietly in his cot at night
My cousin dances with his sister
All day long.

Me and him will go on adventures
In the woods
I love him and he'll love me for evermore.

Maria Katja Heikkilä-Woodhead (9)

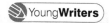

Buddy And Me

Buddy is my special bear
He is unique and rare
He has lots of clothes to wear for fun
I am his dad, he is my son.

He lives in my bed when I'm at school
He does not growl as a rule
I'm so lucky to have a brilliant bear
Who makes me happy and is always there.

Felix Wright (7)

My Dad

S imon is my dad's real name
I like going to the cinema with just me and my dad
M y dad plays football with me
O ne of my favourite people is my dad
N obody is as special to me as my dad.

Callum Payne (7)

My Baby Brother

My baby brother is funny
And he makes me laugh a lot
He's really cute and good-looking
I think he's the best in the world
He's adorable but energetic
Also beautiful and lovely
Don't forget gorgeous and sweet
And he gets sleepy a lot!

Maryam Bint Saqib (10)

My Furry Friend

My favourite furry friend is my cat
Her coat as black as coal
Her whiskers are long and she goes, meow
She's my favourite furry friend

She climbs the trees and even my curtains
She's so sweet
She lets me stroke her head to tail
She's my favourite furry friend.

Sooty, Sooty, she's my little cat
She walks sideways and jumps about
Sooty, Sooty, she's my little cat
She's the cutest thing I know.

She sleeps all day when I am away
She's such a lazy cat
When I get back home she knows it's time
Time to go and play.

She likes her food lots and lots
She always eats a full bowl
I do admire when she gets tired
A sight so cute to see.

Sooty, Sooty, she's my little cat
She walks sideways and jumps about
Sooty, Sooty, she's my little cat
She's the cutest thing I know.

Sooty, Sooty, the cutest thing I know.

Joshua James Whitley (11)

Untitled

He is as scaly as a dragon
His fins swish like a shark
He is as colourful as a peacock
He is as silly as a clown
He is as cute as a kitten
He is my fish, Merlin!

Caitlin Hillier-Kidston (7)

Keira, My Lovely Little Sister

K eira always makes me laugh
E ven when she's in a strop
I love her so much
R oaring like her daddy
A nd she smiles a lot at me

B runch, crunch lunch is coming
R oaring like her daddy
A nd she smiles a lot at me
D addy had the choice of a baby
Y ummy, crunchy Keira.

Charlie Stone (6)
Bowlish Infant School, Shepton Mallet

Holly

H olly is a fun girl
O h, she likes the sea
L olly is her favourite food, we sometimes call her Holly Lolly
L ittle sisters like big sisters
Y es, she is my little sister.

Abbigail Madgett (7)
Bowlish Infant School, Shepton Mallet

Fearne Cotton

F earne is the best, even if famous
E very minute on TV everyone loves her
A beautiful girl
R eally sweet and famous
N ice girl as well
E very day I think of her.

Molly Brooks (7)
Bowlish Infant School, Shepton Mallet

My Favourite Person

M att Smith is fantastic
A t the museum I like to be
T he TARDIS is big on the inside and small on the outside
T he TV is big

S ometimes Matt gets angry
M att Smith is great
I like Matt Smith
T he letter I sent Matt Smith is good
H e is great.

Ashley Williams (7)
Bowlish Infant School, Shepton Mallet

Ronaldo

R onaldo is a right wing player
O n the free kicks he has scored by them
N ow good winger and banger with the ball
A nd he is a very good footballer
L ovely dribbler
D id you know that he could shoot from the halfway line
and hit the crossbar?
O nce he accidentally knocked the goalkeeper out.

Alistair Harrold (7)
Bowlish Infant School, Shepton Mallet

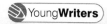

Harvey

H arvey is my best friend
A t playtime he always plays with me
R eally on the PlayStation our favourite game is Harry Potter
V ery often we sit next to each other on the coach
E ven we sit next to each other on the carpet
Y ippeeee.

Seth Biggs (7)
Bowlish Infant School, Shepton Mallet

David Beckham

D avid Beckham might like ham
A nd he is played and paid
V ery good on pitch
I like David Beckham because he scores very good goals
D avid Beckham is a good player but likes haircuts

B eckham is a very, very dear and
E xcellent person at football
C heap haircuts are not right
K icking the ball is just his style
H am could be food he loves
A nd he is a very, very good football player
M en are not like David Beckham.

Zak Withers (7)
Bowlish Infant School, Shepton Mallet

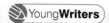

I Love My Best Friend

M olly is my best friend ever
O ff we go to Molly's house, it is fun there
L et's run on I say to Molly
L et's go out of school
Y ou are fun, Molly.

Isabelle Wareham (7)
Bowlish Infant School, Shepton Mallet

Jack

Jack is a close friend of mine
A person who is never mean to me at all
Come on I say and it turns into a fight
We will somehow get back to being friends again
Jack, you are awesome.

Spencer Blake (7)
Bowlish Infant School, Shepton Mallet

Daddy

D ad is funny, happy, joyful
A white van he drives
D ad takes me out every Sunday
D ad is awesome
Y ellow and black, his favourite colours are.

Joe Weller (7)
Bowlish Infant School, Shepton Mallet

My Friend

H arvey always makes me laugh
A nd he is funny and he always lets me play on the PlayStation
R eady to play with me all the time and we sometimes watch
V ideos
E xcited, me after school when I go to Harvey's house
Y ou are fantastic, Harvey.

Jack Byrne (6)
Bowlish Infant School, Shepton Mallet

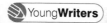

Steven Gerrard

S hoot and score a big goal
T ough luck, you did not score
E ven Ronaldo could not score
V ery hard, I'll tell you now
E very time he's on TV he should score
N ever mind he'll score next time

G ood at all
E ven if it is offside you should continue
R un, run as fast as you can
R ight, let's sort it out
A nd Steven plays for England
R oaring when he misses
D one! We won!

Jack Lintern (7)
Bowlish Infant School, Shepton Mallet

Teacher

My teacher's name is Mrs Zadroznay
She started teaching me when I was nine
She was really funny
And her favourite pet was a bunny.

But unfortunately it came to September
And she didn't blame anyone
So she gave us a penny for good luck
As we travelled all the way to Y6.

Soon as we fitted in with our new class
We waited for our teacher and when we saw him
We all smiled in surprise.

Rachel Burbeary (10)
Coit Friends Club, Sheffield

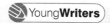

My One In A Million

In the world there's always that one
Who will make you change your ways
Who will turn your world inside out
And shake the foundation of your being.

The one pin in a haystack
The diamond in the mine
The shining star in the sky
They are all one in a million.

You're the greatest treasure
That pearl in the chest
Everyone has their one in a million
Mine, it's well . . .
My sister.

Ifeoma Vania Nwakalor (14)
Corona Secondary School, Nigeria

My One In A Million

My role model, my mentor
The one to look up to
The one that gives joy
The one that teaches me
The one that helps me
To live in harmony.

Appreciation and love
That is what she deserves
The reward of success
I owe her
She provides for me
And keeps me free.

She has done well to me
And I would like to show my affection to thee
I trust you and love you too
You would have shown me that you care.

Ewomazino Osio (11)
Corona Secondary School, Nigeria

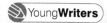

My Role Model

Diligent and caring
Nice and smart
A woman who is an epitome of morality
A God-fearing woman
Eight children and still agile
Never once have heard her say
How mean life is to her
The best advice-giver I know
My first real problem
You were there to help me through it
Although we argued a lot
Doesn't change the fact that
You mean a whole lot to me
Mum, I love you
You are my role model.

Chinonye Ohuruzo (11)
Corona Secondary School, Nigeria

My One In A Million

Felt changes I never thought I could
You brought the good out of me
Made me say things that I never thought I could say
I did the things I never thought I could ever do
You cared when no one seemed to
You kept me strong when everything seemed to be going wrong
You showed me the light
You were always there when it felt like there was no hope
That's why you're my only father, the almighty
My one in a million.

Omonigho Victoria Jatto (14)
Corona Secondary School, Nigeria

My One In A Million

My one in a million
I practically have four
I just don't have one in a million.

My first one in a million
Is my Father in Heaven
And His name is God
God has always been there.

Secondly, my next million
Is my mother
And you can depend on her
And you can always love her.

Thirdly, is just the best
My dad is in his late 40s
A man you can care for
And never forget him.

Lastly and not the least
My sibling that is a boy
A fun, caring and smart one
That is referred to as my brother.

Lydia Adebajo (13)
Corona Secondary School, Nigeria

My One In A Million

Who is she?
Always there for me
Ready to strive in pain
To help make a gain
Who taught me knowledge in all aspects of life
Rendering along love and respect
Showing me the ways of God
And when necessary using a rod
She fills me with love
Just like an angel from above
To you, she may be your one in a million
But to me, she remains my one in a trillion
She is, of course, no other
Than my mother.

Cynthia Okoye (13)
Corona Secondary School, Nigeria

My One In A Million

My one in a million
Is also my hero
My one in a million
Is a very beautiful person inside and outside
Intelligent and caring.

My mother is my one in a million
Not because she is my mother
But she always tries her best to make us happy
Teaches us respect for God
Love, faith in Christ Jesus.

My mother is a blessing sent from above
By God and every day I say thank You
For the parents You gave me
My mother is really my one in a million
She is my star that God always protects.

Everything happens for a reason
But thank God I have someone
Who inspires me to write
My one in a million is and will
Always be my hero
My mother.

Nwaokolo Ruth (12)
Corona Secondary School, Nigeria

One In A Million

My mother
A wonderful person to me
My only one
My companion
Someone I can lean on
My leader
There's no one as special as you are
My one in a million
More precious than gold.

Oluwadara Akinwumi (12)
Corona Secondary School, Nigeria

One In A Million

There are a lot of people on my mind
But the one in my heart is my mother
She makes full joy and happiness
She is like a light in my heart
She is as a devoted mother
Caring, kind-hearted and gentle
Yes, indeed, to me I think she is the one in a million.

Queensly Mbonu
Corona Secondary School, Nigeria

One In A Million

My one in a million
Very hard to find
You can search far and wide
But would run out of time
That's my mum.

Climbing and crawling
Running and jumping
But would not find
Because my heart is where she hides
That is my mum.

All this time I was looking for love
Trying to make things right
But not good enough
I finally decided to quit
But stumbled on you
That's my mum.

Inonekone Eburajolo (12)
Corona Secondary School, Nigeria

The Morning Sky

The sun shines through the sky
Waking animals and such kind
The birds soar, the butterflies flutter
Tulips break ground and the bees buzz around
The earth is moist from the morning dew
Ladybugs fly across the sky
As I look into the sun's eyes.

Jane Vaughn (12)
International School of Geneva, Switzerland

Easter!

He stood anxiously on the staircase listening for the bunny
To his knowing parents this was all rather funny
He stood for a long moment in an eager pose
Before sleep took him and his eyes began to close.
Easter morning began to dawn
And he awakened as the early spring sun blanketed the lawn
The eggs were out there somewhere
Hidden with love and care
He dressed and out the door he flew.
The first egg was easy to find as it was bright blue
The next find was milk chocolate pieces
How did the Easter bunny ever know he loved Reese's?
He found many more treasures
Easter day couldn't have brought any more pleasures!

Catherine Wallace
International School of Geneva, Switzerland

Spring

I am suffocating
Fighting and struggling my way up
Through the warm damp earth

As I push my leaves
Through the crumbling dirt
Small shafts of light stream
Through the cracks

I burst through the ground
Feeling the sun's rays
Beating down on my petals and leaves

Feeling the wind brush and tangle
With my leaves
Hearing the light buzzing of bees
And the sweet joyful chirping of the birds

A feeling of undeniable joy and happiness
Shoots through me
And then explodes like fireworks

To be able to feel and sense
What it is like to be alive again
This feeling only comes
When spring does.

Ivie Orobaton (13)
International School of Geneva, Switzerland

Spring

Flowers chatting
Bees busy
Birds fluttering
Fish alone
Dogs asleep
Trees laughing
Coats disappearing
Books transporting
Sun burning
Me smiling
Spring has arrived.

Sibella Graylin
International School of Geneva, Switzerland

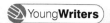

Easter Poem

As I search for my chocolate eggs
I quickly tire my legs
But I won't give up yet
My mom left a set
Easter eggs are yummy for my tummy
And Easter leaves the joy
Nice weather
Blooming flowers
And much more.

Nada Aboul Kheir (11)
International School of Geneva, Switzerland

Spring

As I stepped in the garden
What did I see?
The yellow shining sun smiling at me,
Furry little rabbits hopping around
While tulips and daffodils cover the ground.

Blue skies appear with marshmallow clouds
Children of all ages singing aloud,
White scented blossoms of the apple trees
Flowing through the air in the light spring breeze,
Young lambs skipping in the field
As the swallows fly and sing
They bring the joy of spring.

Ali Atun (12)
International School of Geneva, Switzerland

Children Of The World

This white elegant bunny comes throughout the night
Laying little patterned chocolate out of sight
Then the excited children search right through the town
Hoping their Easter hunt will pay off so they can sit down
Then everyone sitting in their houses all cosy and neat
Will all look like Willy Wonka with a handful of sweets
This will be the first time in the year that kids will be full
But they will be already thinking about next April.

Rory Heppenstall (12)
International School of Geneva, Switzerland

My Favourite Teddy

Rhiana is my favourite teddy
Because in the morning when I rise
I wake up in surprise
I turn my head
Guess what I see?
My favourite teddy, Rhiana
Smiling at me.

Anna McNulty (9)
Lindley Junior School, Huddersfield

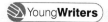

My Favourite Person - Dad

D aring Dad, as he rides his bike across the muddy fields

A wesome Dad as he smashes the ball like a cheetah into the back
  of the net

D ecent Dad as he buys the new DS games because I've been very good.

Jacob Tipple (9)
Lindley Junior School, Huddersfield

Untitled

P owerful Pikachu as strong as a dog
I mportant Pikachu loved very much
K ind Pikachu who wants food all the time
A dorable Pikachu as nice as me
C alm Pikachu as calm as a butterfly
H ungry Pikachu as hungry as a tiger
U ltimate Pikachu, the strongest rabbit.

Kyle Ghulam (8)
Lindley Junior School, Huddersfield

My Favourite Person - Mum

M arvellous, she is good at making weird, different foods
U nderstands us when we tell her something
so she can help us if we have a problem
M y mummy will be over the moon with my school report
as it's good!

Fiza Safdar
Lindley Junior School, Huddersfield

My Dog, Jack

My dog is called Jack and he's black
He won't shake hands
He's black
He won't sit or stay or bark and bay
Or run and play
He won't roll over or shake or crawl
In fact he won't do tricks and that's all
I can tell you about my dog.

Naomii Ely (11)
Weelsby Primary School, Grimsby

My Best Friend

S hannon is my best friend
H appy every day
A nd always there for me
N o one is as special as her
N o one can replace her
O h, the day we go to different schools I will cry
N o one is a better friend than my friend Shannon!

Djamilla Hallam (11)
Weelsby Primary School, Grimsby

My Cat Called Sampson

My cat called Sampson is my best friend
He is the cutest thing I have ever seen
As soon as I get home I get his football out for him
And he never stops batting it all day long
When I go to bed I hear him running
Because his bell tells us where he is.

Mitchell Connor Alder (11)
Weelsby Primary School, Grimsby

My Favourite Person

S hannon is my favourite person
H appy every moment of my life
A nd she is always there for me through good times and bad
N o one is like her
N o one can take our friendship away
O n top of everything she does
N o one in my eyes is as lovely as her
    and that's my favourite person.

Chelsea Long (11)
Weelsby Primary School, Grimsby

My Loving Mum

M um you are my best friend in the world
Y ou mean more than infinity to me

L oving my best friend, it's you
O ther people will always be friends with you
V ery young you are and beautiful
I will always love you
N ever have I been the same without you
G reat love and cute you are

M um I love you more than anything
U sually you're happy and sometimes you're sad
M um you are my best friend.

Aydan Hallam (9)
Weelsby Primary School, Grimsby

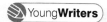

Michael Jackson

M y favourite is Michael Jackson
I like him because he is good at dancing
C an he dance? Oh yes he can
H e is the best dancer in the world
A nd he will show you how to dance
E very day he will practise for his concert
L aughed behind the stage

J uly is the best because it is sunny
A nd he will dance any day for you
C an he do concerts? Oh yes he can
K atie Price likes him
S ometimes he goes into hospital
O n Saturdays he goes there
N ever changes his costume.

Lewis Robinson (8)
Weelsby Primary School, Grimsby

My Best Friend

C ourtney is my best friend
O ur friendship will never end
U nder our skin we know our blood is blue
R unning with each other brings back memories
T he wind blows when we have fun
N ever to tell anyone secrets
E very day we play with each other
Y ou make me feel better when I'm sad

W e never fight with each other
E very time someone bullies us we stick up for each other
R ebecca, me and Courtney always play
R unning and hiding in the trees
E very time we did play it was hide-and-seek
T he wind will start to blow
T he wind will make sure someone will call.

Alicia Hartley (8)
Weelsby Primary School, Grimsby

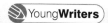

Nanna, You're The Best

N anna you're the best
A nd you're beating all the rest
N anna your nails are as sharp as a dart
N anna, I love you with all my heart
A nd I can't have a nanna as good as you

Y ou to me are the queen of the universe
O h, don't I love you
U nder your shirt is a golden heart
R *oar!* You're not scared of anything
E very day I love you

T ell me the truth that you are the best
H elp is at hand when you are around
E nergetic you are, you're brilliant

B eautiful butterfly
E xcited emu
S lithering snake
T errible tiger.

Elle Mae Barber (9)
Weelsby Primary School, Grimsby

My Mum And Dad

M y favourite person is my mum
Y ou're always there for me

M y mum is special
U nderstands
M y mum is very loving

M y other favourite person is my dad
Y ou're always loving

D ad's the best dad in the whole wide world
A nd he's respectful
D ads are kind and helpful.

Casey Paxton (8)
Weelsby Primary School, Grimsby

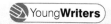

My Dad

M y dad is the best in the world
Y ou will always be there for me

D ad, I will always love you
A ll the time you are there for me
D ad to me is the king of the world.

Tyler Senior (8)
Weelsby Primary School, Grimsby

David Villa

D avid plays for Spain
A ll the time you will be in my mind
V ery smiley you and me together
I will always remember you even when you die
D avid, is the best in my land

V illa, you and Iniesta made your team win
I will meet you one day
L ovely as you are and always will be
L ovely as you are and you will be there
A ll the time I will love you.

Jordan Blackwell (9)
Weelsby Primary School, Grimsby

My Dad

M y dad is kind
Y ou always look after me

D addy is the best
A good dad
D ad is my hero.

Jordan Morley (8)
Weelsby Primary School, Grimsby

My Mum

M y favourite super mum
Y ou're the best mum

M y mum loves me
U sually my mum hugs me
M y mum is my hero.

Owen Lee (8)
Weelsby Primary School, Grimsby

My Mum

M y mum is really good to me
U give me money all the time
M y mum gives me drinks all the time.

Lennox McLellan (8)
Weelsby Primary School, Grimsby

Mum

M um I will love you forever
Y ou are the best mum in the world

M um, I love your so much
U sually you give me the best hugs
M um, you make me happy every year.

Jay Dallow (9)
Weelsby Primary School, Grimsby

YOUNG WRITERS INFORMATION

We hope you have enjoyed reading this
book - and that you will continue to enjoy it
in the coming years.

If you like reading and writing poetry drop
us a line, or give us a call, and we'll send
you a free information pack.

Alternatively if you would like to order further
copies of this book or any of our other titles,
then please give us a call or log onto our
website at www.youngwriters.co.uk

Young Writers Information
Remus House
Coltsfoot Drive
Peterborough
PE2 9JX
(01733) 890066